THREE HUNDRED COPIES
OF THE FIRST EDITION OF
POYNTON PARK
HAVE BEEN SIGNED BY
THE AUTHOR

Robert Manson Myers

EASTER 2005

POYNTON PARK

Books by Robert Manson Myers

HANDEL'S MESSIAH: A TOUCHSTONE OF TASTE (1948)
(New Edition, 1971)

FROM BEOWULF TO VIRGINIA WOOLF (1952)
(New Edition, Revised, 1984)

HANDEL, DRYDEN, AND MILTON (1956)

RESTORATION COMEDY (1961)

THE CHILDREN OF PRIDE (1972)
(New Edition, Abridged, 1984)

A GEORGIAN AT PRINCETON (1976)

QUINTET (1991)

SIXES AND SEVENS (2004)

THE BOSTONIANS (2005)

POYNTON PARK (2005)

POYNTON PARK

A Play in Three Acts

From the Novel

THE SPOILS OF POYNTON

by Henry James

by

ROBERT MANSON MYERS

Charlotte
JOSTENS BOOKS
2005

JOSTENS BOOKS
2400 Crownpoint Executive Drive
Charlotte, North Carolina 28227

To
JUDI DENCH

In the day when the keepers of the house shall tremble....

ECCLESIASTES 12:3

POYNTON PARK

CHARACTERS

Lucy

Fleda Vetch

Mrs. Gereth

Owen Gereth

Mrs. Brigstock

SCENES

The action takes place in the drawing room of Ricks, a country house in Poynton Park, Essex, England, toward the end of the nineteenth century.

ACT ONE

An Afternoon in October

ACT TWO

An Afternoon in November

ACT THREE

An Afternoon in December

Act One

The drawing room of Ricks, a country house in Poynton Park, Essex,
England, on an afternoon in October toward the end of the nineteenth
century. The room is superlatively handsome—spacious, impressive, ex-
quisitely appointed. At the audience's left are double doors leading to the
hall and the other rooms of the house. At the audience's right are French
windows opening onto a terrace, beyond which one glimpses the trees and
lawns of Poynton Park. A fireplace occupies the centre of the rear wall,
and a fire is burning on the hearth. Sofas, chairs, tables, lamps, cabinets,
mirrors, and hangings according to the director's taste and discretion.

During Act One the glow of the afternoon sun gradually fades into
darkness.

At rise no one is onstage. After a few moments LUCY, a parlourmaid, appears in the doorway. She is young and pretty, and a trifle pert in manner
and speech. She is carrying an armful of firewood, which she places in the
woodbin near the hearth. She throws some wood on the fire. Then she pokes
the fire busily, humming a sentimental tune all the while. A bell rings and
she leaves the room to answer it. She is first heard speaking offstage.

LUCY: Afternoon, miss!

(A door slams.)

FLEDA (offstage): Hello, Lucy. I hope Mrs. Gereth's at home?

(FLEDA VETCH appears in the hall. She is an attractive young lady
of twenty-two—pleasant, intelligent, sensitive, refined. She is simply but
tastefully dressed. LUCY helps her remove her things.)

LUCY: Oh, yes, miss! She's been expectin' you since two o'clock.

FLEDA (staring in amazement as she enters the room): Why, Lucy!
This room! It's *beautiful!* It's absolutely *beautiful!*

LUCY (casually): Well, miss, I guess it is, but it certainly ain't
Poynton—if that's what you mean.

FLEDA (uneasily): But, Lucy, I had no idea—

5

LUCY (*interrupting her, as if to avoid the subject*): Beg pardon, miss. I'll tell the lady you're here.

(*As* LUCY *turns to go,* MRS. GERETH *appears in the hall. She is a genuine English lady, fresh, handsome, and young in her mid-fifties, with an air of fatigue on her distinguished face.*)

MRS. GERETH: Fleda, darling! Welcome to Ricks! Welcome to poor little Ricks!

FLEDA (*coming forward*): Mrs. Gereth!

(*The two women embrace.*)

MRS. GERETH: I should have written earlier, I know. But all week I've been too savage even for you.

FLEDA (*uneasily*): I see you've—taken possession.

(LUCY *goes out, leaving the double doors open.*)

MRS. GERETH: Yes, I've come at last—I've crossed the Rubicon! (*Wearily*) It's been like plumping into cold water. But I saw the only thing to do was to stop shivering and take the plunge. (*She pauses to adjust slightly the position of a chair.*) You know, there's more room than I quite measured the other day. And I've found a rather good set of old Worcester. It must have belonged to that maiden aunt—the one who died, years ago, and left this place to Mr. Gereth.

FLEDA (*looking about, with great warmth*): I think I'm already fond of the maiden aunt. She must have been a dear.

MRS. GERETH (*laughing*): Oh, I've quite exterminated the maiden aunt—thank God!

FLEDA (*uneasily*): It's really too wonderful what you've done with the house.

MRS. GERETH (*observing* FLEDA'S *consternation at the room*): Oh, *I* know what you're thinking. (*With extraordinary sweetness and a smile*) But what does it matter *now*, my dear—now that you're on *my* side?

FLEDA (*gasping*): On *your* side! Why, Mrs. Gereth! You've brought away absolutely everything!

MRS. GERETH (*smiling wrily*): Oh, no, you sweet wretch—not everything. (*She goes to the double doors and closes them, as if to ensure privacy.*) I saw how little I could stuff into this scrap of a house. I only brought away what I required.

FLEDA: But you "required" the very best pieces at Poynton!

MRS. GERETH: I certainly didn't want the rubbish, if that's what you mean. Did you really expect me to settle in this dingy little place without a stick of my own?

FLEDA: But, Mrs. Gereth! The place is simply *crammed!* (*She moves about the room, admiring its beauties.*) The Venetian lamp—the Italian cabinet—that old Spanish altar-cloth—those Louis Quinze brasses—even the Maltese cross! (*She picks up a Maltese cross from the table and examines it.*)

MRS. GERETH (*sharply*): "Even" the Maltese cross! My dear child, you don't suppose I'd have sacrificed *that!*

FLEDA: But how in the world did you get off with all these things?

MRS. GERETH (*magnificent in her triumph*): Oh, I was crafty! I manœuvred. I chose my time. And then at last I rushed! (*She slowly rubs her hands.*) Oh, I was horribly extravagant—I had to turn on so many people. I haven't paid for it yet—there'll be a horrid bill. But at least the thing's done! "I can give you two days," I said. "I can't give you another second." The men came down on Tuesday morning; they were off on Thursday. Oh, I admit some of them worked all Wednesday night. You know, my dear, I'm quite remarkable. I lifted tons with my own arms. (*Wearily*) Now I'm very, very tired. (*Brightening*) But there's not a scratch, not a nick, not a teacup missing! (*She laughs ironically.*) Upon my word, I do believe they really look better here!

FLEDA (*awe-struck*): And no one at Poynton said anything? There was no alarm?

MRS. GERETH: What alarm *could* there be? Owen hasn't been at Poynton for nearly a month. (*Suddenly she grasps* FLEDA'*s question.*) You mean I was watched—you mean Owen hired servants to telegraph him if they saw what I was up to? Precisely—*I* know the scoundrels you have in mind. (*She laughs.*) I settled *them* all right! I put them to work. I marched up and looked each one straight in the eye. I gave each one his chance to choose between me and my son. And each one chose to help *me!* Oh, they were too stupid!

FLEDA (*with mounting apprehension*): And when did all this take place?

MRS. GERETH (*unperturbed*): Only last week—it seems like a hundred years. Of course, I'm not really settled yet—you'll see in the rest of the house. But, thank God, the worst's over. (*She goes to the fireplace and begins to poke the fire.*)

FLEDA (*gravely*): Do you really think so? I mean—does Owen accept it all now that it's done?

MRS. GERETH (*casually*): Owen? I haven't the slightest idea.

FLEDA: Does Mona?

(*This question is more serious.* MRS. GERETH *turns from the fireplace to address* FLEDA.)

MRS. GERETH: You mean *she'll* be the soul of the row?

FLEDA (*drily*): I hardly see Mona Brigstock as the "soul" of anything. But you've heard nothing at all?

MRS. GERETH: Not a whisper, not a step, in all eight days. (*Ironically*) Perhaps they don't know. Perhaps they're crouching for a leap!

FLEDA: But wouldn't Owen have come down to Poynton as soon as you left?

MRS. GERETH: How should *I* know? How should *I* know anything at all? Perhaps he's at Colonel Gereth's in town. Perhaps he's at Waterbath, shooting wild duck with Mona Brigstock. You know Owen. From the first he's failed to understand what it means to have a mother. Why, I'm just his mother, don't you see—just as his nose is simply his nose! (*Warming with her theme*) Gracious goodness! One's mother! Why, one's mother's a subject for *poetry!* Look at how Frenchmen treat women in my position—women no better than me. Take my friend Madame de Jaume. Each of her three boys wrote to her every day of their lives! She kept her house in Paris; she kept her house in Poitou. Till the end of her days she had the final word about everything. (*Bitterly*) But Owen?

Why, Owen's never shown me the least gallantry. From boyhood he's never shown me the least tenderness. (*Reminiscently*) Two years ago, when Mr. Gereth died, everything at Poynton went straight to his son. (*She speaks now with a sort of tragic violence.*) And here I am, condemned to spend my declining years in this miserable cottage on the grounds of Poynton Park. (*She sighs.*) But after all, how could my husband guess that the heir to the loveliest house in England should feel inspired to hand it over to a Waterbath Brigstock?

FLEDA: *Some* people, you know, might *see* something in Mona. (*She sits down on the sofa.*)

MRS. GERETH (*groaning with disgust*): Mona Brigstock? Oh, my *dear*! (*She shakes her head.*) No, Fleda, Owen's never taken the least pride in his house. Didn't you see his den at Poynton? It's monstrous—all tobacco-pots and mooseheads and bootjacks, with eighteen rifles and at least forty pistols and God knows how many horsewhips!

FLEDA: Well, then—if he doesn't care, he'll give them up.

MRS. GERETH: Give what up?

FLEDA: Why, all these beautiful things.

MRS. GERETH (*bitterly*): To whom? To that unspeakable product of Waterbath?

FLEDA: To you, of course—to keep for yourself.

MRS. GERETH (*sharply*): And leave Poynton as bare as your hand?

FLEDA: I don't mean he'd give up *everything*. But surely he'd let you have the few things you like best.

MRS. GERETH: *Like best!* There isn't a thing in the house I don't like best!

FLEDA: But certainly he'd let you keep *something!*

MRS. GERETH (*considering*): I think he *would* if he were free.

FLEDA: You mean *she'll* prevent him?

MRS. GERETH: By every means in her power!

FLEDA: But surely not because she appreciates them!

MRS. GERETH: How could a Waterbath Brigstock appreciate

anything? Why, last summer at Poynton she wandered through the corridors like a bored tourist. Her eyes might just as well have been blue beads! (*She mocks* MONA'*s voice.*) "At Waterbath," she said, "we may not have a library, but at least we have a billiard room." (*She frowns with disgust.*) Oh, she's brutally ignorant—that's plain enough—a mere bundle of petticoats.

FLEDA: Then why won't she give them up?

MRS. GERETH: Because they belong to Poynton, and Poynton belongs to Owen. If I tried to take *anything* she'd say, "It goes with the house!" Day after day she'd repeat it—the shameless hoyden—in that voice like the squeeze of a doll's stomach: "It goes with the house! It goes with the house!"

FLEDA: But can't something be *arranged?* Can't you go on living at Poynton?

MRS. GERETH (*laughing bitterly*): With Mona Brigstock? Do you really see *me* spending the rest of my days with that vicious creature's elbow halfway down my throat? How could I sit there an instant and endure *her* horrors?

FLEDA: Well, after all, she wouldn't smash things—she wouldn't burn them up.

MRS. GERETH: But she'd neglect them; she'd ignore them; she'd leave them to clumsy servants. And then she'd mix them with those maddening relics of Waterbath—those cheap little blue plates, those hideous wall brackets with the pink vases, those bunchy draperies, those souvenirs, those family photographs, those—what-do-you-call-'em—those grease-catchers! (*Woefully*) I ask you—could Fate really saddle me with a daughter-in-law brought up in such a place?

(*The double doors open and* LUCY *enters.*)

LUCY: Beg pardon, mum, but Mr. Owen's waitin' in the library.

MRS. GERETH (*stunned*): Mr. Owen!

LUCY: He just now come down from Waterbath, mum.

MRS. GERETH (*trying to conceal her apprehension with good humour*): Well! I *thought* it would be *somebody*, but I rather expected a *lawyer.* (To LUCY) For whom did he ask?

Fleda (*quickly*): For you, of course, Mrs. Gereth!

Lucy (*indifferently*): He asked for Miss Vetch, mum.

Mrs. Gereth: Of course. Fleda, you must go to him.

Fleda: Oh, no, Mrs. Gereth! I couldn't possibly face Owen now. Not in this house—not with all these—these spoils of Poynton!

Mrs. Gereth (*dismissing* Lucy): Tell him Miss Vetch will come.

(Lucy *goes out, leaving the double doors open.*)

Fleda: But, Mrs. Gereth! What on earth can I do?

Gereth: What you always do—see what he wants. He's right to ask for you—he knows you're still our go-between. Nothing's happened to change *that*. If he's come to say—

(*Suddenly she sees* Owen Gereth *standing at the door. He is a tall, handsome, sport-loving young Englishman twenty-four years old. He is manly but shy, slow-witted but affable.*)

Owen (*smiling brightly*): Hello, Mummy.

Mrs. Gereth: Owen!

(*There is an awkward silence as* Owen *kisses* Mrs. Gereth. *All three characters remain standing.*)

Owen (*eagerly*): Good afternoon, Miss Vetch!

Fleda (*pleasantly*): Hello, Mr. Gereth. I was just coming to the library.

Owen (*smiling*): But it's much nicer here, don't you think? (*Suddenly pained*) Of course, I didn't quite expect— (*He gazes about the room in consternation.*) You see, I've just come from Waterbath and—

Mrs. Gereth (*a bit too brightly*): Waterbath? Well, well, well, my dear boy—how *is* Miss Brigstock?

Owen (*absently*): Oh, she's all right.

Mrs. Gereth: And what *does* your young friend there make of our little odds and ends?

Owen (*absently*): Oh, she thinks they're all right.

Mrs. Gereth (*more seriously*): But has she any sort of *real feeling* for nice old things?

Owen (*casually*): Oh, of course—she likes everything that's nice.

Mrs. Gereth (*with passionate intensity*): I think I could give up everything—without a pang—to a girl I could trust—to a girl I could *respect*. For twenty-six years your father and I collected these things. We worked for them, we waited for them, we suffered for them. Yes, we almost starved for them! They were our religion, they were our life, they were *us!* And now they're only *me*, except that they're also partly *you*, my dear! (*She puts her arm about* FLEDA*'s shoulder and gives her a playful little shake. Then she turns to* OWEN *with tragic intensity.*) There wasn't a thing at Poynton I didn't know and love. Blindfold, in the dark, with the brush of a finger, I could tell them apart. But now—rather than hand them over to a Waterbath Brigstock—I think I'd deface them with my own hands. I think I'd *burn* them piece by piece! (*She is now almost in tears.*) I couldn't *bear* the thought of such a woman at Poynton! I *couldn't!* Who'd save my treasures for me—I ask you who *would?* (*She turns to* FLEDA *with a dry, strained smile.*) *You* would, of course—only you, in all the world—because *you* feel, *you* understand, *you* care! *You* would replace me, *you* would watch over them, *you* would keep the place right. With *you* there I think I might rest at last in my grave! (*She turns to* OWEN.) If you'll take *her* I'll send back every piece without a sound. But if you take anyone else—heaven help me, I'll fight to the death!

(MRS. GERETH *sweeps out into the hall, leaving* FLEDA *and* OWEN *speechless with surprise and embarrassment.* FLEDA *is about to follow* MRS. GERETH *when* OWEN *proceeds to close the double doors. During the following scene with* FLEDA *he seems rather too punctilious for a man known to be engaged to another woman.*)

OWEN: Well! I'm glad *that's* over! (*He sighs.*) You know, I'm afraid we're in for an awful row.

FLEDA: An awful row?

OWEN: Mummy and I. She thinks Mona's a regular barbarian.

FLEDA (*with much warmth*): Why, Mona's *lovely!*

OWEN (*casually*): Oh, well—*she's* all right. Mummy must come round.

FLEDA: Of course she must. And she *will*, I know. Only give her time.

OWEN: She can't keep me waiting forever, you know. Naturally I want my own furniture.

FLEDA (*smiling*): "Furniture"! You make it sound like mattresses and washstands!

OWEN: "Works of art," then. You know my father made every arrangement for me to have them. Of course, if there are a few pieces Mummy likes best, I'd let her take them without a word.

FLEDA (*drily*): Subject, of course, to Miss Brigstock's approval. (*She sits down on the sofa.*)

OWEN: You don't think I'm being rough or hard, do you? After all, Ricks here is an awfully jolly little place. Mona took a tremendous fancy to it.

FLEDA: Indeed? Has Mona seen Ricks?

OWEN: She saw it last summer. She thinks Mummy's awfully lucky to be here. She thinks Mummy's making it devilish awkward about the things. I suppose you know she's taken everything—at least a lot more than I ever dreamed. You can see for yourself— she's got half the place down. (*Inarticulate, he resorts to his old trick of artless repetition.*) You can see for yourself! (*He sighs.*) If she thinks I *like* it—! (*Ruefully*) And we left it all to her honour!

FLEDA: Perhaps you've a right to say you left it partly to *mine*.

OWEN (*quickly, almost pleading*): You don't really think it's fair, do you?

FLEDA (*hesitantly*): I think she's gone too far. I shall immediately tell her I've said that.

OWEN (*puzzled*): Then you haven't told her what you think?

FLEDA: I only got here this afternoon. I had no idea what she was doing. She managed it wonderfully.

OWEN: It's the sharpest thing *I* ever saw! (*He laughs bitterly.*) Poor dear old Mummy! That's why I asked for you—to see if you'd back her up.

FLEDA: How can I back her up, Mr. Gereth, when I think she's made a great mistake? Of course, there are many things she *hasn't* taken.

OWEN: Just the same, you'd hardly know the place at Poynton. I was there this afternoon. (*He gazes about the room.*) But you'd know *this* place soon enough, wouldn't you? These are just the things she ought to have left. Is the whole house full of them?

FLEDA: The whole house.

OWEN (*sadly, still gazing about the room*): I never knew how much I cared for them. They're awfully valuable, aren't they? Mummy thinks I never took any notice, but I was awfully proud of everything.

FLEDA: Of course you were! I shall instantly let your mother know the way I've spoken to you.

OWEN: You'll tell her what you think she ought to do? (*He fidgets about the room with his hands in his pockets.*) *Don't* you think she ought to give them up?

FLEDA: Is that what you came to say?

OWEN: Not exactly those words. But I *did* come to say—I *did* come to say we must have them right back.

FLEDA: And did you think your mother would see you?

OWEN: I wasn't sure, but I thought I'd try. Of course, I'd much rather see you than her. In fact, I don't really want to see Mummy at all. I only came down today because I don't want Mummy to think I haven't been all right. If she won't see me, of course—well, I *could* have sent down the lawyers.

FLEDA (*startled*): I'm glad you didn't do *that!*

OWEN: I'm dashed if I *want* to! But, hang it, Miss Vetch, what's a fellow to do? If she won't meet a fellow—

FLEDA: What do you call meeting a fellow?

OWEN: Why, letting *me* tell her what she can have.

FLEDA: And if she won't do that?

OWEN: Well, I'll leave it to my solicitor. *He* won't let her off, by Jove! I *know* the fellow!

FLEDA: But that's *horrible!*

OWEN: It's utterly beastly.

FLEDA (*considering*): Is Mona very angry?

OWEN: Oh, dear, yes! She hates it awfully. (*He is standing with his back to the fireplace, his legs apart, his hands behind him.*) She won't put up with it at all. You see, she saw the place with all the things.

FLEDA: So of course she misses them now.

OWEN: Misses them—rather! She was awfully sweet on them. As Mona says herself—it's just as if I'd obtained her under false pretenses. She thinks it's a regular *sell!*

FLEDA: When does the marriage take place?

OWEN (*uneasily*): It's a little uncertain. The date isn't quite fixed. (*He crosses from the fireplace to the window.*)

FLEDA: I thought you told me last summer it might come off later this month.

OWEN (*gazing out of the window*): I daresay I did—it was for the twenty-eighth. But we've changed that now—Mona wants to shift the date. (*He turns suddenly from the window.*) In fact, it won't come off at *all* till Mummy sends back the things.

FLEDA: Oh? (*There is a pause.*) Then you want me to tell your mother you demand immediate restitution?

OWEN: Please. It's tremendously good of you.

FLEDA (*rising from the sofa*): Very well, then. Will you wait?

OWEN (*perplexed*): For Mummy's answer? Don't you think she'll hate it worse if I'm here? Won't she think I'm trying to make her reply bang off?

FLEDA: You aren't, then?

OWEN: I'm trying to be fair, don't you know? I want to give her more than just an hour or two.

FLEDA: Then if you don't want to wait— (*She moves toward the door.*)

OWEN: Must *you* do it bang off?

FLEDA: I'm only thinking she'll be impatient—I mean, to know what's passed between us.

OWEN: But there's really no need to rush. I mean—I can give her a day or two, you know. (*He pauses a moment.*) Of course, I didn't come down to sleep. If I'd known *you* were here I might have stayed over. I mean—I could talk with *you* a blessed sight longer than I could with Mummy.

FLEDA (*smiling*): We've already talked a long time.

OWEN: Awfully, haven't we? But please, Miss Vetch—please don't say anything about Mona.

FLEDA: Mona?

OWEN: About its being *her*, I mean, who thinks Mummy's gone too far. That would only make Mummy worse.

FLEDA: Certainly I won't *mention* Mona. And it won't be at all necessary.

OWEN (*confidentially*): You know, Miss Vetch, it's awfully nice of you to look after me and poor Mummy this way. I do hope you'll stay on a while. Poor Mummy's always happier with a—a companion in the house. And if anything's to be done I know you're just the one to do it. I can't tell you how it feels to know you're on *my* side!

FLEDA: Up to this time your mother's had no doubt of my being on *hers*.

OWEN: Then of course she won't like your changing.

FLEDA: I daresay she won't like it at all!

OWEN: You mean you'll have a regular kick-up with her?

FLEDA: We'll have some lively discussion—if that's what you mean. Remember—for your mother to make a public surrender of what she's publicly—taken will go pretty hard with her pride.

OWEN: I suppose she's tremendously proud, isn't she?

FLEDA: You know better than I.

OWEN: I don't know anything in the world better than you! If I were half as clever as you I might hope to get round her. In fact, I don't quite see what even *you* can do to *really* bring her round.

FLEDA: Neither do I—as yet. All I can say is—I'll try. (*Earnestly*) I *want* to try, you know—I *want* to help you. (OWEN *stands looking at her in silence.*) So now you must leave me—alone with her, I mean. You must go straight back.

OWEN: Back to Waterbath?

FLEDA: Oh, no—back to town. I'll write you tomorrow at Colonel Gereth's.

OWEN (*turning vaguely to go*): There's a chance, you know, she may be afraid.

FLEDA: Afraid, you mean—of the lawyers?

OWEN: I've got a perfect case—I could have her up. The Brigstocks say it's downright stealing.

FLEDA (*drily*): I can easily guess what the Brigstocks say!

OWEN: It's none of their business, is it?

FLEDA: They've a much better right to say it's none of *mine!*

OWEN: Well, at any rate, *you* don't call Mummy names.

FLEDA: You don't know *what* I'll call her if she holds out!

OWEN: But suppose she's angry at you for backing me up—what will you do then? You won't go away, I hope?

FLEDA: Go away? Everything depends. You must wait and see. (*She moves toward the door.*)

OWEN (*still not satisfied*): You want me to go, and I'll be off in a minute. Only—before I go, please answer me one question. If you *should* leave my mother, where would you go?

FLEDA: I haven't the least idea.

OWEN: I suppose you'd go back to town?

FLEDA: I haven't the least idea.

OWEN: You don't—uh—live anywhere in particular, do you?

FLEDA (*ignoring this awkward question*): I *won't* leave your mother. (*Resolutely*) I'll persuade her—I'll convince her absolutely.

OWEN: I believe you *will* if you look at her like that! (*He is now standing between* FLEDA *and the door, with his hand on the knob, smiling strangely.*) You know, Miss Vetch, when I got into this squabble I didn't know you; and now that I *do* know you—now that I *do* know you—Mona seems so different, so—well— (*Pleading*) Listen, can't something be done?

FLEDA (*struggling for self-control*): *Please,* Mr. Gereth! I *must* get on! (*As* OWEN *opens the door* LUCY *is seen passing in the hall.*) Oh, Lucy! Has Mrs. Gereth come in?

LUCY: No, miss. But I think she's left the garden, miss. I think she's gone up the back road—to Poynton.

FLEDA: Thank you, Lucy. Would you please show Mr. Gereth out.

LUCY: Yes, miss. (*She disappears into the hall.*)

OWEN (*lingering awkwardly*): You know, I think it's awfully nice here. I think I could do with it myself.

FLEDA (*laughing*): I should think you *might*—with half your things here! It's Poynton itself—almost.

OWEN: Oh, I don't mean with all the things here. I mean I could put up with it just as it *was*. It had a lot of good things, don't you think? (*He is close to her now.*) I mean—if everything was back at Poynton, I could live here with *you*. Don't you see what I mean?

FLEDA (*desperately maintaining self-control*): *Please*, Mr. Gereth, I— (*She is almost in tears.*) Good-bye, Mr. Gereth. (*She proffers her hand.*)

OWEN (*holding her hand firmly*): There's one thing I suppose I ought to tell you, since you're good enough to see Mummy for me—but of course you'll see it's something it won't do to tell *her*. (*He pauses nervously.*) It's just that I understand from Mona—it's just that she's made no bones about bringing home to me—well, if I don't get the things back—every blessed one of them except a few *she'll* pick out—she won't have anything more to say to me!

FLEDA (*astonished*): Why, Mr. Gereth!

OWEN (*his voice wavering*): She simply won't *have* me, don't you see? (*He releases her hand at last.*)

FLEDA (*bravely*): Oh, never mind, Mr. Gereth—*you'll* get the things. You *will*, I'm sure of it. You're quite safe—don't worry! Good-bye! (*She waves him into the hall.*) Good-bye!

(FLEDA *turns back into the room, smiling in her new joy. She picks up the Maltese cross from the table and examines it musingly. Then, the cross still in her hand, she moves to the window, where she stands gazing at Poynton in the growing darkness as* LUCY *returns.*)

LUCY: Well, miss—so he's gone. (*She proceeds to light a lamp.*) Strange, ain't it—him runnin' off so quick-like! And without so much as a how-de-do to his pore mother.

FLEDA (*firmly*): You'd better bring tea, Lucy. (*She looks out of the window.*) I see Mrs. Gereth coming up the garden path.

LUCY: Of course, miss. (*She starts to go.*) Awkward for you, miss, ain't it? I mean—havin' to keep peace between Mr. Owen and—and the lady. Everybody in the kitchen says— (*She breaks off suddenly as she sees* MRS. GERETH *rushing in from the terrace.*) Good evenin', mum. (*She disappears into the hall, leaving the double doors open.*)

MRS. GERETH (*breathlessly*): Well, my dear—so he's come and gone! (*She drops her things on a chair.*) I saw him leaving just now through the front gate. What did he have to say for himself?

FLEDA (*bursting forth suddenly*): Oh, Mrs. Gereth, how *could* you? Great God! How *could* you?

MRS. GERETH (*blankly*): What on earth do you mean? How could I *what*?

FLEDA: How could you fling me at Owen's feet that way?

MRS. GERETH (*genuinely surprised*): Why, Fleda! Don't you *want* to be shown off to Owen as the right sort of wife for him? Why not, in the name of wonder, when you *are* the right sort? (*Tenderly*) You know, my dear, I've taken a tremendous fancy to you. Ever since we first met—last spring at Waterbath—you've been under my wing—first in town, then at Poynton, and now—

FLEDA (*almost defiantly*): Mrs. Gereth, I've half a mind to leave Ricks this very instant.

MRS. GERETH (*unaware of her rudeness*): But, my dear child—where could you go?

FLEDA: Why, to my father's place in town. Since Mother's death last year he's had rooms in West Kensington.

MRS. GERETH (*almost contemptuously*): But you haven't a penny to your name!

FLEDA (*turning away sadly*): I know—it's terribly inconvenient. But Father pays some of my bills—even though he won't take me in to live with him. (*Brightening*) And after Maggie's wedding, of course, there'll always be *her* little house in Surrey.

MRS. GERETH: Maggie? Is your sister engaged to be married?

FLEDA: Didn't you know? It's coming off quite soon—early in December, I think. She's engaged to a curate. In any case—

MRS. GERETH (*with finality*): In any case, you'll be so good as to stay right here with me. (*There is a pause.*) After all, my dear—you *would* marry him, wouldn't you—if that Waterbath creature weren't there? (*An afterthought*) I mean, of course, if Owen were to *ask* you.

FLEDA (*indignantly*): Most decidedly not!

MRS. GERETH: Not even to have Poynton?

FLEDA (*almost too emphatically*): Not even to have Poynton!

MRS. GERETH: But why on earth?

FLEDA (*searching for a reason*): Because—because—he's engaged to be married to Miss Brigstock!

MRS. GERETH (*laughing*): Oh! Is *that* all he came to say?

FLEDA (*firmly*): He came to demand that you send back everything as fast as the vans will carry it.

MRS. GERETH (*sharply*): Oh! (*She sits down.*) Quite a "demand," dear, isn't it?

FLEDA (*smiling wrily*): It's what *I'd* call *coercion!*

MRS. GERETH (*quickly*): What sort of coercion?

FLEDA: Why, legal, of course. He's ready to set the lawyers at you.

MRS. GERETH (*laughing*): Oh, the lawyers! Is he going to send them down here?

FLEDA: He thinks it may come to that.

MRS. GERETH (*drily*): The lawyers can scarcely do the packing. (*There is a pause.*) Did he seem angry?

FLEDA (*tenderly*): He seemed sad. He takes it very hard.

(FLEDA *sits down on the sofa, where she remains seated during the remainder of Act One.* MRS. GERETH, *on the other hand, moves about the room constantly, now and then adjusting the position of a chair.*)

MRS. GERTH (*probing*): And how does *she* take it?

FLEDA (*faltering*): Oh, that—*that* I hesitated to ask.

MRS. GERETH: So you didn't get it out of him?

FLEDA: I didn't think you'd care.

MRS. GERETH: Is that what you told him?

FLEDA: I told him I think you're—very obstinate and very proud.

MRS. GERETH: Quite right, my dear. I'm a rank bigot—about this sort of thing! (*She indicates the furnishings of the room.*) I'd kidnap the children of heretics—to save them. When I know I'm right, I go to the stake. (*Majestically*) Oh, he may burn me alive! (*Suddenly, after a pause, she begins probing again.*) Did he abuse me?

FLEDA: How little you know him!

MRS. GERETH (*laughing oddly*): Ah, my dear—certainly not so well as *you!* (FLEDA *turns away self-consciously.*) Why did you "hesitate," as you say, to speak of Mona?

FLEDA (*with dignity*): I should think *you* would know.

MRS. GERETH: Because I "threw" you at his feet? Because I told him you were the one? You *were*—you are still!

FLEDA (*with a bold, dramatic laugh*): Thank you, my dear—with all the best things at *Ricks!*

MRS. GERETH: For *you*, you know, I'd send them back.

FLEDA: For *me?* Why in the world for *me?*

MRS. GERETH: Because you're so awfully keen.

FLEDA: Am I? Do I strike you so? (*A bit too vehemently*) You know I *hate* him!

MRS. GERETH (*sternly*): Then what's the matter with you? Why do you want me to give in?

FLEDA (*uneasily*): I've only said your *son* wants it. I haven't said *I* do.

MRS. GERETH (*peremptorily*): Then say it and have done with it!

FLEDA (*with growing uneasiness*): I'm only thinking of Owen's engagement.

MRS. GERETH: His engagement to marry? Why, it's just that engagement we *loathe!*

FLEDA (*with a strained voice*): Why should *I* loathe it? I'm simply thinking of his original understanding—to give Mona the house with all the things.

MRS. GERETH (*outraged*): *To give Mona the house!*

FLEDA (*more positively*): I'm thinking of the simple question of his keeping faith. I'm thinking of his honour—his good name.

MRS. GERETH: The honour and good name of a man you hate?

FLEDA (*resolutely*): Certainly. I don't see why you should talk as if I had a petty mind. I can do your son justice—just as he puts his case to me.

MRS. GERETH (*triumphantly*): Then he *did* put his case to you! You spoke just now as if nothing passed between you.

FLEDA: Something always passes when there's a little imagination.

MRS. GERETH (*laughing*): I take it you don't think Owen has any. (*Abruptly*) Why is it you hate him so?

FLEDA (*hesitantly, searching for an answer*): Should I love him for all he's made you suffer?

MRS. GERETH (*moved*): Fleda, darling! (*She goes to* FLEDA *and speaks with great tenderness and warmth.*) No, my dear, you haven't a petty mind. You've a lovely imagination, and you're the nicest creature in the world. If you were silly, like most girls, I'd have insulted you, I'd have outraged you—you'd have fled from me in terror, you'd have told people I'm a brute. You're very clever, my dear, and very patient. (*Suddenly she breaks out with renewed determination.*) But does it strike you he really believes I'd give way?

FLEDA: I think he really believes if I try hard enough I can *make* you.

MRS. GERETH: And you've promised to try—I see. You didn't tell me *that* either. But you're rascal enough for anything! (*Suddenly*) At any rate, why the devil doesn't it come off?

FLEDA (*simply*): You mean their marriage?

MRS. GERETH (*violently*): Of course I mean their marriage!

FLEDA: I haven't the least idea.

MRS. GERETH (*probing*): You didn't ask him? What were you doing all that time?

FLEDA (*shocked*): Oh, how in the world can you think—?

MRS. GERETH: Think of your asking a question so indelicate? *I* should have asked it—in your place, I mean. But *I'm* quite coarse—thank God! (*With increasing purpose*) What, then, *was* the day to be?

FLEDA: I'm sure I don't remember.

MRS. GERETH: Isn't the day past? (*Suddenly she stops short.*) Gracious goodness! They must have put it off! (*She eyes* FLEDA.) *Have* they put it off?

FLEDA (*nervously*): I haven't the least idea.

MRS. GERETH (*insistent*): Didn't he tell you—didn't he say anything about it?

FLEDA: He told me nothing whatever. He didn't *mention* his marriage.

MRS. GERETH: Not in any way?

FLEDA: Not in any way.

MRS. GERETH (*looking hard at* FLEDA): You haven't a notion they're waiting for the things?

FLEDA: How *should* I have? *I'm* not in their counsels.

MRS. GERETH (*considering*): I'll wager they are—at least, Mona is. (*Suddenly she springs up.*) Upon my word, if I don't give in, I'll be hanged if she won't break off!

FLEDA (*shaking her head*): She'll never, never break off.

MRS. GERETH: Are you sure?

FLEDA: It's my belief.

MRS. GERETH (*impatiently*): Oh, it's an awful bore you didn't really get it out of him! (LUCY *enters carrying a tray and places the tea-things on a table in front of* FLEDA.) Well, here's tea. Thank you, Lucy. (FLEDA *proceeds somewhat absentmindedly to prepare tea. As she shovels tea into the pot* MRS. GERETH *gently reproves her.*) Not *five*, my dear—the usual three. (*By now it is totally dark outside. During the ensuing conversation* LUCY *lights another lamp, draws together the curtains, picks up* MRS. GERETH'*s things from the chair, and goes out, leaving the double doors open.*) You haven't told me, you know, how you propose to "make" me.

FLEDA: Give everything back? Why, by being so eloquent I'll persuade you. By making you sorry you went so far. By reminding you it's the first thing I've ever asked of you. Oh, you've done things for me—beautiful things, but I've never so much as *asked* you for a postage stamp.

MRS. GERETH (*imperiously*): Give me a cup of tea. (FLEDA *pours a cup of tea and hands it to* MRS. GERETH, *who by now is seated on the sofa beside* FLEDA. *For a moment* MRS. GERETH *stirs her tea in silence.*) No, my dear, you've never asked me for a postage stamp.

FLEDA (*half playfully*): And *that*, you see, gives me a pull! (*She pours herself a cup of tea.*)

MRS. GERETH: You mean—makes you expect me to do this thing simply to oblige you?

FLEDA: You said a while ago you *would* do it—for *me.*

MRS. GERETH: Yes, my dear—for *you* I'd return the things—all of them. But you haven't told me what you'd do in return.

FLEDA: Anything in the wide world.

MRS. GERETH: Oh, "anything" is nothing at all! It's too easily said.

FLEDA: Well, then, try me with something. What is it you ask?

(MRS. GERETH *places her teacup on the table with a decisive gesture, springs up suddenly, and speaks with great intensity.*)

MRS. GERETH: *Get him away from her!*

FLEDA: Away from Mona? How in the world—?

MRS. GERETH (*sharply*): By not looking like a fool! I say, don't look like an idiot, because you happen not to be one—not the least bit. *I'm* idiotic, God knows! I've *been* idiotic, I see now—ever since we first met. I've been a precious donkey! (*She goes to the fireplace and begins poking the fire violently.*)

FLEDA: *How* can I get Owen away from Mona?

MRS. GERETH: By cutting in! By letting yourself go!

FLEDA (*blankly*): By letting myself go?

MRS. GERETH (*turning from the fireplace, poker in hand*): My dear child, you've done two things this afternoon you've never done before. You've asked me to do you this favour, this service, this—whatever-you-call-it. And you've told me an immense little fib!

FLEDA (*stupefied*): An immense little fib! (*She puts down her teacup.*)

MRS. GERETH (*moving about the room, wielding the poker ominously*): An immense *big* one, then! You don't in the least "hate"

Owen, my dear. You care for him very much. In fact, my dear, you're in *love* with him! There—don't tell me any more lies!

FLEDA (*horrified*): Lies!

MRS. GERETH: Oh, you're a wonder—you're magnificent! I was right, as soon as I saw you, to pick you out and trust you. I never dreamed of it till a while ago. After he'd come and gone—when you and I were face to face—something stuck out of you. You'd just been with *him*, and you weren't natural—you weren't natural to *me!*

FLEDA: But, Mrs. Gereth—

MRS. GERETH: And then suddenly it all dawned on me when you said you'd asked him nothing about Mona. It put me on the scent. But I didn't show you, did I? I felt it was *in* you, deep-down—I felt I must draw it out. Well, I *have* drawn it out, and it's a blessing. (*She returns the poker to the fireplace.*) Why, Fleda, it isn't a crime—don't you know that? When I was a girl I was always in love—and not always with such nice people as Owen. (*Passionately*) *Save* him, Fleda—*save* him! You *can!* How could you *not* like him when he's such a dear? You can do what you want with him—you know you can! *Get him away from her!* Don't abandon him—poor wretch—to such a fate, and *I'll* never abandon *you*. (*She is almost in tears.*) Think of him with that creature, that family, that future! If you'll take him I'll give up everything. There—it's a solemn promise, the most sacred of my life. Get the better of *her* and he'll have every stick I grabbed. Give me your word, and I'll write for the packers tonight!

FLEDA: My dear Mrs. Gereth, you see more in this thing than can ever be.

MRS. GERETH: I see in it simply what *must* be, if you've a single spark of pity!

FLEDA: But after my hideous double game how can you ever believe in me again?

MRS. GERETH: Where on earth was the double game? You've behaved like a saint!

FLEDA (*simply but firmly*): I couldn't possibly do what you ask.

Mrs. Gereth (*staring at* Fleda): Why, in the name of goodness, when you adore him so?

Fleda: He cares for *her* too much.

Mrs. Gereth: *Then why the deuce doesn't he marry her?*

Fleda: He doesn't dream I've ever *thought* of him. Why *should* he if you didn't?

Mrs. Gereth (*laughing*): It wasn't *me* you were in love with, my duck! (*With sudden decision*) *I'll* go and tell him.

Fleda (*firmly*): Mrs. Gereth, if you do any such thing you'll never see me again—absolutely never!

Mrs. Gereth (*looking hard at* Fleda): Then you're perverse—you're wicked. Will you *swear* he doesn't know?

Fleda (*indignantly*): Of course he doesn't know!

Mrs. Gereth: Will you swear he has no feeling on *his* side?

Fleda (*horrified*): For *me?* Before he's even married her?

Mrs. Gereth: Oh, my dear—you *are* a treasure! Doesn't Owen appreciate *anything*—the great gawk? He's given you absolutely no sign?

Fleda (*firmly*): Absolutely none.

Mrs. Gereth: Then he's as big a donkey as his mother! (*There is a pause.*) But you know, you've got to account for their delay.

Fleda: Why have I "got" to?

Mrs. Gereth: Because you were closeted with him so long this afternoon—on this very spot. Mona or no Mona, do you think Owen could see you this way—utterly alone—and not have the ordinary feelings of a *man?* Don't you know what men *are*—the brutes? You know, my dear, you can't pretend to have no art!

Fleda (*debating*): Perhaps their delay may be—Mona's doing. I mean—because she's lost the things.

Mrs. Gereth (*jumping at this*): So she'll break altogether if I keep them?

Fleda (*desperately*): Oh, no, Mrs. Gereth! She'll make scenes—she'll worry him. But she'll hold him fast—she'll never let him go.

Mrs. Gereth (*triumphantly*): Upon my word, I *will* keep them! I'll keep them just to try Mona Brigstock!

FLEDA: Is that what you want me to write him?

MRS. GERETH: Write him that you must see him again.

FLEDA (*blankly*): What on earth am I to see him for?

MRS. GERETH: For anything you like!

FLEDA: Are you suggesting that I ask him to come down here?

MRS. GERETH: Dear no! Say you'll go up to town to meet him. Deal with him in your own way—I ask no questions. All I ask is that you put it through.

FLEDA: But that's no answer to Owen's message.

MRS. GERETH: My answer to his message is perfectly clear. He'll have everything back at Poynton the minute he says he'll marry *you*.

FLEDA: And you really think *me* capable of writing him that news?

MRS. GERETH: What else can I think—when you threaten so to cast me off if I write him myself?

FLEDA (*rising at last from the sofa*): Mrs. Gereth, how can I go on living with you this way—thinking as I do you've plundered Owen so unmercifully? How can I stay here without feeling I'm backing you up in your cruelty? (*As if to go*) In a day or two, you know, I'll hate every object in this house!

MRS. GERETH (*imperturbable*): It's too beautiful, my dear, the way you care for him—it's music in my ears! Nothing else but such a passion could make you say such things. (*She goes to* FLEDA, *who is now nearing the door.*) Why didn't you tell me sooner? I'd have gone right in for you—I'd never have moved a candlestick. Don't stay with me if it torments you. Go back to town—go back to your father's place for a couple of weeks. He'll be glad to take you in—if you'll only make him see it's a question of getting *you* off his hands forever. Your chance is in town, my dear. For God's sake, use it! If you're in need of money, I think I can spare a little. (*She puts her arm around* FLEDA, *and together they pass into the hall.*) Only let yourself go, darling—only let yourself go!

(MRS. GERETH'*s last words may be heard offstage as the curtain slowly falls.*)

Act Two

An afternoon in November. The drawing room is brilliant with the glow of the afternoon sun, which gradually fades into darkness.

At rise FLEDA VETCH *is seated on the sofa reading* The Morning Post. *She is dressed almost gaily, and somehow she seems prettier, more radiant than in Act One. In a moment* MRS. GERETH *appears. She is carrying a bowl of flowers, which she sets down on a table.*

MRS. GERETH: Well, my dear—any word in *The Morning Post?*

FLEDA (*not looking up from her newspaper*): No word about the wedding—if that's what you mean.

MRS. GERETH (*triumphantly*): There! You see? Nothing! Not a word! Don't tell *me!* It's been more than a month, and still he doesn't breathe a word about the *day!* All three weeks in town you didn't hear a whisper—not a syllable! Nothing could be plainer than this silence. It simply speaks volumes. It proves I'm settling Mona.

FLEDA (*looking up from her newspaper*): You may be settling Mona, but are you settling Mona's lover?

MRS. GERETH (*standing at the table, arranging the flowers*): Why not? It's perfectly clear their marriage is practically off. (*Suddenly she shivers.*) Good heavens! It's cold in here! (*She calls.*) Lucy! Lucy! (*Half to herself*) Where the devil is that girl anyway? (*She goes to the door and shouts into the hall.*) Lucy! Lucy! (*She turns back into the room.*) What do you suppose those monsters at Waterbath are doing?

FLEDA (*putting her newspaper aside*): The Brigstocks? I suppose they're waiting—waiting to see what *you* do!

(LUCY *appears in the doorway.*)

MRS. GERETH (*sternly*): Lucy, why haven't you built up this fire?

LUCY (*distressed*): Oh, mum—I *did* build up the fire. This mornin', mum. I was most particular—

MRS. GERETH (*more sternly*): Lucy, how many times have I told you—in weather like this—?

LUCY: Oh, yes, mum—I know, mum. But—well—you see, Mr. Owen's waitin' in the library and—

MRS. GERETH (*gasping*): Mr. Owen! Good God, girl—why didn't you *tell* me?

LUCY: Well, mum, I—

FLEDA (*stunned*): How long has he been here?

LUCY (*as if to reassure her*): Oh, he just now come down from London, miss.

MRS. GERETH (*half to herself*): Well, you know, I rather expected he'd be down today. (*She starts to go.*) Show him in *here*, Lucy. (*An afterthought*) And you'd better bring tea.

LUCY: For three, mum?

MRS. GERETH: For *two*, of course.

LUCY: Yes, mum. (*She goes out.*)

FLEDA (*appalled at the prospect of another tête-à-tête with* OWEN): But, Mrs. Gereth—

MRS. GERETH (*peremptorily*): Talk to him, Fleda—see what he wants. Do as you've done before.

FLEDA (*with rising tension*): But, my dear Mrs. Gereth—

MRS. GERETH (*grabbing a coat lying on a chair*): As far as *I'm* concerned, if I couldn't face him a month ago, how can I face him today?

(MRS. GERETH *disappears through the terrace door, leaving* FLEDA *in great agitation.* FLEDA *dashes to a mirror, before which she pauses to check her appearance. In a moment* OWEN *enters from the hall.*)

OWEN (*cheerfully*): Well, Miss Vetch—good afternoon!

FLEDA (*pleasantly*): Hello, Mr. Gereth. You've taken us quite by surprise!

OWEN (*awkwardly*): Well, I've been wanting awfully to see you again. And then yesterday Mummy wrote that you were back at Ricks.

FLEDA: So you've reopened relations with her!

OWEN: Oh, no—*she's* reopened relations with *me*. (*He pulls out a letter.*) She's still a bit nasty. Listen. (*He reads.*) "Fleda Vetch is back at Ricks. Come down to see her and try, for God's sake, to cultivate a glimmer of intelligence." (*He laughs uncomfortably.*) That's a good one for me, isn't it?

FLEDA: Of course you know by this time your mother's very direct. (*She sits down on the sofa.*)

OWEN: If you don't mind my saying so, Miss Vetch, I think you've been keeping me pretty well in the dark. Can't Mummy say what she'll do, one way or the other? I don't know where I stand. I don't really know where *she* stands. You wrote me to be patient, and I'd like to know what else I've been. But you don't realize what I have to be patient *with*. At Waterbath, don't you see, I have to account for all this damned furniture—piece by piece. Mona glares at me and waits—and, hang it, Miss Vetch, I glare at *you* and do the same. I hope you've not been keeping anything back from me all this time.

(LUCY *enters carrying a tray and places the tea-things on the table in front of* FLEDA. *As* FLEDA *and* OWEN *continue speaking she goes out, closing the double doors behind her.*)

FLEDA: Oh, no—I've been trying to break your mother down. She's too proud to change all at once, but I think I've made an impression. Anyway, now that I've done all I can, I'm getting on back to town.

OWEN (*surprised*): But, Miss Vetch! I thought you'd come down for the winter!

FLEDA: Oh, no—I can't stay. Maggie's wedding comes off in December. Besides, I don't like what your mother's done. Here in the midst of all this plunder—all these trophies of Poynton—living with them, touching them, using them every day—I feel as if I'm backing her up. (*She returns to* OWEN*'s question.*) I haven't written because I've been hoping to learn something more from your mother. (*She begins to make tea.*)

OWEN: And you've learned nothing at all?

FLEDA: Not a thing.

OWEN: Then you and Mummy have quarrelled.

FLEDA: Oh, no—we haven't quarrelled a bit! (*She smiles.*) We've only—diverged.

OWEN: Then you've diverged pretty far! You've had a row with her and still you haven't moved her!

FLEDA: I think the trouble is—she can't see why your wedding doesn't come off.

OWEN: Why, that's simple. Mona won't take another step till Mummy's given full satisfaction. Everything must go back to Poynton—every blessed thing she stole.

FLEDA: You told me that before. But I haven't told your mother. You can easily see why. Even so, I think she has her suspicions. She thinks if she holds off long enough she may put an end to your engagement. She thinks if Mona's waiting she may tire Mona out.

OWEN (*with a strange approach to hilarity*): So far as that goes, she *has* tired Mona out.

FLEDA (*astonished*): You mean your marriage is off?

OWEN (*with the oddest sort of gay pessimism*): God knows, Miss Vetch, *what* I mean! If it isn't *off* it certainly isn't *on*. I haven't seen Mona for ten days; I haven't heard a thing for over a week. And she used to write me every day! She won't budge from Waterbath, and I haven't budged from town. (*There is a pause.*) If she *does* break, will Mummy come round?

FLEDA (*hesitating*): If your marriage really drops, I think she'll give up everything.

OWEN: That's just what makes Mona hesitate!

FLEDA: Hesitate to keep you—or hesitate to give you up?

OWEN: She doesn't see any use in hanging on. You see, I haven't even called in my lawyer. She's awfully keen on that; she's awfully disgusted that I haven't. She says it's the only real way, and she thinks I'm afraid. She says I give Mummy too much time. She says I'm a muff to go pottering on. That's why she's drawing off so hard, don't you see?

FLEDA: I don't see very clearly. But of course you *must* keep your word—of course you *must* give her what you promised. There must be no mistake about *that!*

OWEN: Then you think I *must* send down the police?

FLEDA: Oh, no—not yet! If Mona's drawing off, as you say, she may have a very high motive. She knows the great value of all these beautiful things. Perhaps she's ready to—to sacrifice her engagement in order to restore them to Poynton.

OWEN: Oh, but Mona's not that sort! She wants them herself—she wants to feel they're *hers*. She doesn't care whether *I* have them or not. And if *she* can't get them she doesn't want *me*.

FLEDA: She takes such an interest in them?

OWEN: So it appears.

FLEDA: So much that she lets everything else depend on them?

OWEN: She never *really* wanted them till they seemed to be in danger. *Now* she has an idea about them, and when Mona gets hold of an idea—! (*He gazes out of the window with an expression of futility. Then suddenly he turns.*) I say, you know, *do* give me some tea!

FLEDA (*laughing awkwardly*): Oh, of course. How stupid of me! (*She pours a cup of tea.*)

OWEN: No cream, please.

FLEDA: Here you are. (*She hands the cup to* OWEN.) Am I to understand that Mona engaged herself to marry you without caring for you? (*She pours herself a cup of tea.*)

OWEN: She *did* care for me awfully. But she couldn't stand the strain.

FLEDA: The strain of what?

OWEN: Why, of the whole wretched thing.

FLEDA: The whole thing *has* been wretched—I can easily understand how she feels.

OWEN (*surprised*): You *can*? (*He turns around sharply.*) You can understand her coming down on *me*? She acts as if I'm no use to her at all!

FLEDA: She's rankling under a sense of wrong.

OWEN (*with unaccustomed heat*): Well, was it *I*, pray, who *did* the wrong? Haven't I done all I could to get the thing settled?

FLEDA: You've been perfect. You've had a difficult job, and I've not helped at all.

OWEN: Well, *you* wouldn't have stopped liking me, would you? I mean—if you *had* liked me—liked me the way *she* liked me.

FLEDA (*embarrassed*): I can answer that better if I know how *kind* you've been. *Have* you been kind?

OWEN: I've done every blessed thing she ever asked! Last month I rushed down here to Ricks with fire and sword, and the day after that I went straight to Waterbath. (*He puts down his teacup.*) Well, *shall* I tell my lawyer to act?

FLEDA (*ignoring his question*): When you went to Waterbath after seeing me here, did you tell her all about that?

OWEN: "All" about it?

FLEDA: That you'd had a long talk with me—alone.

OWEN: Oh, yes—I told her everything. I told her you'd been awfully kind. I told her I'd placed the whole thing in your hands.

FLEDA: Perhaps *that* displeased her.

OWEN: It displeased her fearfully. She wanted to know what right you had to meddle. She said you weren't—honest.

FLEDA (*wailing*): Oh! (*She controls herself.*) I see. (*She puts down her teacup.*)

OWEN: She abused you. She denounced you—

FLEDA (*rising and checking him with a gesture*): Don't tell me *what* she did! (*With a forced smile*) You spoke a while ago about my quarrelling with your mother about *you*. The truth is—you and Mona have quarrelled about *me!*

OWEN: If you don't mind my saying so, Miss Vetch, I think Mona's jealous.

FLEDA: Well, I suppose our talks *have* looked rather odd.

OWEN: They've looked very beautiful. And they've *been* very beautiful. Oh, I've told her the sort *you* are!

FLEDA (*drily*): That, of course, hasn't made her love me any better.

OWEN: No—and it hasn't made her love *me* any better either. So far as that goes, of course, she *says* she loves me.

FLEDA: And do you say you love *her?*

OWEN: I say nothing else—I say it all the time. I said it just the other day about fifty times. (*There is a pause.*) Well, *shall* I tell my lawyer to act?

FLEDA (*ignoring his question*): You tell me you "say" you love her. You wouldn't say so, would you, if it weren't true? What in the world's become of the feeling that led to your engagement?

OWEN: The deuce knows *what's* become of it, Miss Vetch! It all seemed to go to pot when this horrid squabble came on. (*He is close to her now.*) As I noticed you more, as I came to know you better, I felt less and less for Mona. I began to wish I'd known you sooner—I'd have liked you better than anyone else in the world. But it wasn't *you* who made the difference—it was Mona. All the time she wanted to know what was going on between us—between you and me; and she wouldn't take my solemn word that nothing was going on except what might have gone on between me and old Mummy. She said a pretty girl like you was a nice old Mummy for me, and she never called you anything else but that. I'll be hanged if I haven't been good, haven't I? I haven't breathed a word to you, have I? You'd have been down on me hard if I had, wouldn't you? You're down on me pretty hard as it is, aren't you? But I don't care *what* you say to me now—or what Mona says either. I don't care a single rap what anyone says. After her confounded behaviour I've a right to speak my mind. (*With great firmness*) And I'm saying right now it had all better come to an end. You ask me if I don't love her—I suppose it's a natural question. But you ask it at the very moment I'm half-mad to say there's only one person on the whole earth I *really* love, and that person— (*There is a sound of voices in the hall.* FLEDA *tries to break away, but* OWEN *is holding her close.*) You can certainly guess—you can certainly guess the one person on earth I *really* love!

FLEDA (*struggling to free herself from* OWEN's *embrace*): *Please*, Mr. Gereth! *Please!* Your mother!

(*Suddenly* LUCY *opens the double doors.*)

LUCY (*whispering excitedly*): Oh, miss! There's a lady in the front hall—askin' for you. Name of Brigstock.

FLEDA (*aghast*): Brigstock!

OWEN: Mrs. Brigstock! Here?

(FLEDA *and* OWEN *look at each other in amazement as* MRS. BRIGSTOCK *edges past* LUCY *and strides into the room. She is an imperious, over-dressed woman in her mid-fifties. For a moment she stares first at* FLEDA *and then at* OWEN. *Then she studies the contents of the room, finally bringing her eyes to rest on* FLEDA'S *handkerchief, lying suggestively on the carpet at* OWEN'S *feet.* OWEN *somewhat sheepishly stoops down, picks it up, and hands it to* FLEDA. *Composing herself at last,* FLEDA *goes to* MRS. BRIGSTOCK, *extends her hand, and breaks the awkward silence.*)

FLEDA: Mrs. Brigstock! We're—we're just now having tea.

MRS. BRIGSTOCK (*coldly*): Indeed. Then please don't let me intrude. I came on the mere chance. I thought I might find you here. (*She sits down on the sofa.*) But of course if I didn't find *you* I thought perhaps I might find Mrs. Gereth.

(LUCY *goes out, leaving the double doors open.*)

FLEDA (*nervously*): Oh, yes—she—she's spending the day at Poynton. (*She sits down on the sofa.*)

MRS. BRIGSTOCK: All day long?

FLEDA: Well—most of it.

MRS. BRIGSTOCK: Leaving you here quite to yourself?

FLEDA: A good deal to myself—yes. But a little this afternoon to Mr. Gereth.

MRS. BRIGSTOCK (*coldly*): So I see. In fact, I'm afraid I've interrupted your conversation. You must be very much taken up—I mean with his dreadful quarrel.

FLEDA (*vaguely*): His dreadful quarrel?

MRS. BRIGSTOCK: About the furniture. Aren't you looking after all these things for him?

OWEN (*almost too eagerly*): You see, Miss Vetch, she knows how awfully kind you've been.

FLEDA (*calmly*): Please understand, Mrs. Brigstock—I'm here only at Mrs. Gereth's request. She asked me particularly to see Mr. Gereth for her.

MRS. BRIGSTOCK: And did she ask you particularly to see Mr. Gereth here at Ricks?

OWEN: Mrs. Brigstock, I made a point of letting Mona know I'd be here today, don't you see? That's exactly what I wrote her this morning. But of course the letter hadn't arrived when you left Waterbath.

MRS. BRIGSTOCK: She'd have had little doubt you'd be here with Miss Vetch if you had half a chance. If your letter *had* arrived, of course, it might have prepared me for finding you two here—so engrossed in your tea. In that case I certainly wouldn't have come.

FLEDA (*simply and sincerely*): Then I'm glad it didn't arrive. Wouldn't you like Mr. Gereth to leave us?

MRS. BRIGSTOCK (*glaring at* OWEN *and considering*): I'd like Mr. Gereth to come with *me!* (*Her eyes return to* FLEDA.) I've not seen him for weeks. I've particular things to say to him.

OWEN: So have *I* particular things to say to *you*, Mrs. Brigstock. (*He moves as if to go.*)

MRS. BRIGSTOCK (*to* FLEDA): What's Mrs. Gereth going to do?

FLEDA: Is that what you came to ask me?

MRS. BRIGSTOCK: That and several other things.

FLEDA (*affably*): Then you'd much better let Mr. Gereth go, and stay by yourself and make a pleasant visit. You can talk with him whenever you like.

MRS. BRIGSTOCK: I *can't* talk with him whenever I like! He hasn't been *near* us since I don't know when! But there are things that brought me here.

OWEN: They can't be things of any importance. You know, Mrs. Brigstock, I don't think you should come down on Miss Vetch about anything. It's very good of her to take the smallest interest in our vulgar little squabble. If you want to talk about anything, talk with *me*. I don't like your cross-questioning her. She's as straight as a die.

MRS. BRIGSTOCK (*to* FLEDA): Upon my word, he speaks as if I'd come here to be rude to you!

FLEDA (*nervously*): I'm not in the least afraid to be alone with you, Mrs. Brigstock. I'll answer any question you can possibly dream of asking me.

OWEN (*with unaccustomed firmness*): *I'm* the proper person to answer Mrs. Brigstock's questions, and I'm not a bit less prepared to answer them than you are.

FLEDA: But she'll only have been here a few minutes. What sort of visit is that?

MRS. BRIGSTOCK (*sharply*): I think it's lasted long enough for my purpose. There was something I wanted to know, but I think I know it now.

OWEN: Anything you don't know I daresay I can tell you!

FLEDA (*earnestly*): Mrs. Brigstock, there may be things you know that I don't, but I've a feeling you're labouring under some great mistake.

OWEN: She probably is, Miss Vetch. But there's no one in the world to whom *you* owe an explanation.

FLEDA (*sweetly*): But what if there's one it's no trouble at all for me to give? (*She faces* MRS. BRIGSTOCK.) I'm sure it's the only one Mrs. Brigstock came to ask.

MRS. BRIGSTOCK (*with passionate intensity*): I came, Miss Vetch— I believe I came just—you know—to *plead* with you.

FLEDA (*half-amused*): To *plead* with me? As if I were one of those bad women in a play?

(*This remark is disastrous. There is an awful silence.* MRS. BRIGSTOCK *is visibly offended. She rises grandly from the sofa and moves toward* OWEN.)

MRS. BRIGSTOCK: I'm quite ready. I do want to speak to you very much.

OWEN: I'm completely at your service.

FLEDA (*distressed*): But, Mrs. Brigstock— (*She rises from the sofa.*)

MRS. BRIGSTOCK (*coldly*): Good afternoon, Miss Vetch. (*She sweeps out into the hall.*)

FLEDA (*in anguish*): Mr. Gereth!

OWEN: I'll be back as soon as I can. You mustn't worry, you know—you mustn't! Wait for me—I'll be back!

(OWEN *goes out. For a moment* FLEDA *stands motionless; then she moves to the table, picks up the Maltese cross, and examines it musingly. A door slams, and in a moment* LUCY *appears.* FLEDA *returns to the sofa, where she takes up her embroidery.*)

LUCY: Well, now—ain't *she* the royal one! You'd of thought it was the Queen herself! (*Mocking, with exaggerated gestures*) "I'm quite ready. I do want to speak to you very much." Ain't it awful, miss—about the things, I mean? Honest, when I think o' Poynton in the hands o' that Brigstock woman! When's it comin' off anyway, do you think?

FLEDA (*trying to seem casual*): The wedding? Mr. Gereth's wedding? I haven't the least idea.

LUCY: Well, miss, if you don't mind *me* sayin' so, it ought to be *you* that's gettin' married to Mr. Owen. (*She begins poking the fire.*)

FLEDA (*laughing*): Why, Lucy! How you talk!

LUCY: But he *do* like you, don't he, miss?

FLEDA: How on earth should *I* know? I'm far too much taken up with my *sister's* wedding!

LUCY (*interested*): Miss Maggie, you mean? Miss Maggie and the parson?

FLEDA: I'm going up to town next week to help with Miss Maggie's clothes. The wedding's December third. But if you keep talking, Lucy, I won't have this embroidery done in time.

LUCY (*with deepening interest*): Oh, miss! A gift for the bride? (*She examines the embroidery.*) Now, ain't that nice! (*She sighs romantically.*) Well, I wish 'em luck—with all my heart I do.

FLEDA: Has Mrs. Gereth come in yet?

LUCY: She's takin' a turn in the park, I think, miss. Prob'ly waitin' till Mr. Owen clears out. (*She is at the window.*) Why, here comes Mr. Owen now! Why, miss, he's comin' back! I'd better go find the lady—before she pops in here unawares.

(LUCY *takes the tea-things and goes into the hall, leaving the double doors open. In a moment* OWEN *runs in from the terrace, breathless and smiling.*)

OWEN: *Well,* Miss Vetch! I'm practically a free man!

FLEDA (*astonished*): A free man! What did Mrs. Brigstock say?

OWEN: Oh, she was horrid—we had a beastly scene. (*Shivering, he goes to the fire to warm his hands.*) I knew what she wanted to say—that's why I got her off. She brought it out as soon as we left the house. She asked me point-blank if I was in love with you.

FLEDA (*alarmed*): And what did you say to *that*?

OWEN (*smiling*): I said it was none of her business.

FLEDA (*drily*): I'm not so sure!

OWEN: Well, *I* am, and *I'm* the person most concerned. Of course, I didn't use just those words—I was perfectly civil. But I told her I didn't think she had a right to ask me any such question. I said the whole thing was between Mona and me, and if she didn't mind, it would just have to stay that way.

FLEDA: All that didn't answer her question.

OWEN: You think I should have told her?

FLEDA (*laughing*): I think I'm rather glad you didn't!

OWEN: Oh, I knew what I was about. She has no right to come down on us that way.

FLEDA: When she first arrived she probably didn't mean to "come down."

OWEN: Then what *did* she mean to do?

FLEDA: What she said to me just before she left—she meant to *plead* with me.

OWEN: Plead with you for what?

FLEDA: For you, of course. Plead with me to give you up. She thinks I'm awfully designing—she thinks I've taken some sort of possession of you.

OWEN: You haven't lifted a finger! *I'm* the one who's taken possession!

FLEDA: Yes—but it's enough for *her* that we're so—intimate.

OWEN: *I* am, but *you're* not!

FLEDA (*ignoring his remark*): When she found you here, looking so much at home, paying me a friendly call and shoving the tea-things about—it was just too much for her patience. She simply made up her mind on the spot—she thinks I'm a very bad case. (*She lays aside her embroidery and rises from the sofa.*)

OWEN: Do you know what she had the cheek to ask me? She asked me in a sort of nasty way if I thought you "really" cared anything for me. Of course I said you didn't—not a solitary rap. But I could see she thought I lied. She said our relation—yours and mine—isn't innocent.

FLEDA (*alarmed*): What did she mean by that?

OWEN: She said it's jolly unnatural!

FLEDA: Well, it *is!*

OWEN: Then it's only because *you* make it so! I mean—by keeping me off.

FLEDA (*sweetly*): Have I kept you off today?

OWEN (*taking* FLEDA's *hand*): Miss Vetch—Fleda—dear Fleda— you're beautiful—you're more beautiful than anyone, but I'll be hanged if I can ever understand you. (*Tenderly*) You shine at me like an angel, but it doesn't bring you an inch closer to saying what I want you to say. (*Fervently*) What I want you to say is you *like* me. What I want you to say is you'll *save* me!

FLEDA: Why do you need saving if you're a free man?

OWEN: It's just *because* I'm free. Don't you see what I mean? Fleda, dearest—I want you to marry me. (*He moves to embrace her, but she avoids him.*)

FLEDA: First let me know what you mean by your "freedom." I gather Mrs. Brigstock wasn't wholly satisfied with the way you answered her question.

OWEN: Well, the less *she's* satisfied the more *I'm* free.

FLEDA: What bearing have *her* feelings, pray?

OWEN: Why, Mona's much worse than her mother, you know. She's much more anxious to give me up.

Fleda: Then why doesn't she do it?

Owen: She will, as soon as her mother gets home and tells her.

Fleda: Tells her what?

Owen: Why, that I'm in love with *you!*

Fleda: Are you so very sure she will?

Owen: Certainly I'm sure. And *that* will finish Mona!

Fleda: Can you take such pleasure in her being "finished"—a poor girl you once loved?

Owen: I don't think I ever *really* loved her, you know.

Fleda (*laughing*): Then how am I to know you "really" love—anybody else?

Owen: Oh, I'll show you that!

Fleda: So I must take it on trust. And what if Mona *doesn't* give you up?

Owen: Why, that's just where *you* come in.

Fleda: To save you? You mean *I* must get rid of her for you? (*She smiles wrily.*) You see, Mr. Gereth—you see how impossible it is to talk of such things yet!

Owen (*grasping her arm*): You mean you *will* talk of them? You *will* listen to me? When? When?

Fleda (*suddenly bursting into tears*): When it isn't simply agony!

(*At last* Fleda *breaks down in* Owen's *arms. He draws her close and kisses her.*)

Owen (*tenderly*): Fleda, darling! All this time you cared?

Fleda (*sobbing*): Of course I cared! How could I *not* care? (Owen *kisses her again. Then she breaks away.*) But you must never, never ask me again. It isn't for us to talk about. Don't speak of it—don't speak!

Owen (*ecstatically*): Now I'm ready for anything! I have your word.

Fleda: We mustn't talk—we mustn't! We must wait! (*Half in tears, she speaks with passionate intensity.*) Everything must come from Mona. If it doesn't come from Mona we've said entirely too much. You must leave me alone—forever.

Owen (*gasping*): *Forever!*

FLEDA: Unless everything's different.

OWEN: Everything *is* different—now that I know you!

FLEDA: You *don't* know me—you don't! Go back to town and wait! You mustn't break down at this point.

OWEN: I'll find a letter from Mona tonight.

FLEDA: So much the better if it's the kind of letter you want.

OWEN: But suppose there *is* no letter?

FLEDA: You mean—suppose she doesn't let you off? Oh, you ask me too much! How can *I* tell you? What do *I* know? If she doesn't let you off it's because she's still attached to you.

OWEN: She's not—she's not! You can take it from me she loathes me.

FLEDA: Then why doesn't she prove it in the only clear way?

OWEN: She *has* proved it. Will you believe me if you see the letter?

FLEDA: I don't want to see any letter. You'll miss your train.

OWEN (*taking her hand*): Do you mean to tell me I must marry a woman I hate?

FLEDA: You see it's not true that you're free! It's not true!

OWEN: Do you mean to tell me I must marry a woman I hate?

FLEDA (*gasping*): No. Anything's better than *that!*

OWEN: Then in God's name what must I do?

FLEDA (*speaking in broken bits*): You must settle that with Mona. You mustn't break faith. Anything's better than *that!* She *must* love you—how can she help it? (*She is almost panting now.*) You offered her marriage. It's a tremendous thing for her. *I* wouldn't give you up! Never, never, never!

(*Hysterically* FLEDA *grasps* OWEN'*s hand and presses it to her lips. Then* OWEN *kisses her tenderly. Finally* FLEDA *breaks away and* OWEN *disappears into the hall, leaving the double doors open. For a moment* FLEDA *stands motionless. After a pause she returns to the sofa and bursts into tears. In a moment* MRS. GERETH *bounds in from the terrace.*)

MRS. GERETH (*brightly*): *Well,* my dear—everything's settled at last! We're leaving right after Christmas—you and I—we're taking a little trip!

FLEDA (*trying to collect herself*): Why, Mrs. Gereth! I'm not in the least prepared to take a trip!

MRS. GERETH: Then you'll be so good as to make preparations on the spot! (*She drops her things on a chair. During the following scene* FLEDA *remains seated on the sofa, while* MRS. GERETH *darts vivaciously about the room.*) You're going abroad with *me.*

FLEDA: Going *abroad!*

MRS. GERETH (*with calm finality*): That's all that's left for us now. I've made my plans—we go for at least a year. Of course I don't expect you to stay with me *all* that time. We'll go straight to Florence. Owen will join us as soon as possible. Oh, I'm convinced it's the right thing to do. It'll make a nice change—it'll put in a decent interval.

FLEDA: And you really have it from Owen that he'll join us?

MRS. GERETH: Oh, if *you'll* answer *for* him it'll do quite as well! (*With a knowing smile*) You bad, false thing—why didn't you *tell* me? You *must* have known, and yet you practically denied it!

FLEDA (*blankly*): What on earth are you talking about?

MRS. GERETH: You've done everything you need for modesty, my dear! Owen's sick with love for you—and you don't need *me* to tell you!

FLEDA: Has he told *you*, Mrs. Gereth?

MRS. GERETH: How *could* he when he communicates with me only through you, and you're so tortuous you conceal everything?

FLEDA: Then how do you know your son has ever thought—

MRS. GERETH: That he'd give his ears to get you? (*She laughs triumphantly.*) I've had a visit from Mrs. Brigstock!

FLEDA (*amazed*): She saw you too?

MRS. GERETH: In the garden—ten minutes after she found Owen at your feet. (*Almost amused*) She knows everything!

FLEDA (*shaking her head sadly*): There are things Mrs. Brigstock doesn't know!

MRS. GERETH: She knows he'd do anything to marry *you!*

FLEDA: He hasn't told *her* so.

Mrs. Gereth: No—but he's told *you*. That's better still! My dear child, don't try to make yourself out better than you are. I haven't known you so long for nothing. You're not quite a saint in heaven yet. Lord, what a creature you'd have thought *me* in *my* good time!

Fleda (*considering*): You know, I'm surprised Mrs. Brigstock thought it would help her to see you.

Mrs. Gereth: You should never be surprised at born fools. If a cow tried to calculate, that's the kind of happy thought she'd have. Mrs. Brigstock came down to *plead* with me.

Fleda: That's what she came down to do with *me*. But what did she hope to get from *you*—with your opposition so open from the first?

Mrs. Gereth: She didn't know I want *you*, my dear. It's a wonder—with all my violence! But she's as stupid as an owl—she doesn't feel your charm.

Fleda: Did you tell her about my charm?

Mrs. Gereth: What do you take me for? I wasn't such a booby!

Fleda: Did she come down to complain of me?

Mrs. Gereth: She came down to see what she could do. She didn't really mean to see *me* at all, but she was tremendously upset by what she saw this afternoon. The whole story, she said, was written on your two faces. Owen was on the brink—she might still save *him*. "What *won't* a mother do?"—that was one of the things she said. What won't a mother do indeed! I thought I'd already shown her what! She tried to break me down by appealing to my good nature, as she called it. And from the moment she started on *you*, my dear, I was as good-natured as she could ask. It was a plea for mercy pure and simple—because you and Owen were killing her child. Of course I was delighted to have Mona killed, but I was scrupulously kind to Mrs. Brigstock. I asked her why the marriage hadn't taken place weeks ago, when Owen was perfectly ready. I showed her it was Mona who'd killed *him*—it was Mona who destroyed *his* affection. She said she didn't come down to get the things back—she came simply to get Owen. She asked me point-blank if I could possibly want him to marry *you.*

FLEDA (*gasping*): And what did you say to *that?*

MRS. GERETH: I saw my danger—the danger of her going home and telling Mona I was backing you up. I said her question showed a total misconception of my present relations with Owen. I told her nothing has passed between Owen and me for weeks.

FLEDA: And was Mrs. Brigstock satisfied with your answer?

MRS. GERETH: She was obviously relieved. At least she left— thank God!—thinking she'd got something.

FLEDA: And what *did* she get?

MRS. GERETH: Nothing—except a walk in Poynton Park. But *I* got everything!

FLEDA: Everything?

MRS. GERETH: You dear old wretch! Don't fail me now!

FLEDA (*suddenly pained*): What on earth have you done?

MRS. GERETH: I've *settled* you—I've arranged to send everything back!

FLEDA (*stupefied, rising from the sofa*): Back to Poynton? Everything?

MRS. GERETH (*magnificent*): Everything—straight down to the smallest snuffbox!

FLEDA (*desperately*): Oh, no, Mrs. Gereth! No! You must wait! You must wait!

MRS. GERETH (*riding over her*): The last load goes back Friday. I've engaged the same people to do it. Poor little Ricks will soon be empty! See what I do for *you,* my dear? Now what will you do for *me?* (*She starts to go but turns as she nears the door.*) They're *yours,* you silly goose—they're *yours!*

(MRS. GERETH *smiles and rubs her hands as the curtain slowly falls.*)

Act Three

An afternoon in December. The appearance of the drawing room is strikingly altered. Most of the handsome pieces seen throughout the first two acts have been replaced by pieces of much greater simplicity. The former atmosphere of splendid elegance is now an atmosphere of homelike charm. If anything, the room is more pleasant now than before.

During Act Three the glow of the afternoon sun gradually fades into darkness.

At rise no one is onstage. After a few moments LUCY appears in the doorway. She is carrying an armful of firewood, which she places in the woodbin near the hearth. She throws some wood on the fire. Then she pokes the fire busily, humming a sentimental tune all the while. A bell rings and she leaves the room to answer it. She is first heard speaking offstage.

LUCY: Afternoon, miss!

(A door slams.)

FLEDA (offstage): Hello, Lucy. I hope Mrs. Gereth's at home?

(FLEDA VETCH appears in the hall. She is simply but tastefully dressed. LUCY helps her remove her things.)

LUCY: Oh, yes, miss! She's been expectin' you since two o'clock.

FLEDA (staring in amazement as she enters the room): Why, Lucy! This room! It's beautiful! It's absolutely beautiful!

LUCY (casually): Well, miss, I guess it is, but it certainly ain't Poynton—if that's what you mean.

FLEDA (with great enthusiasm): Oh, no! It's much nicer than Poynton! So much nicer! And so much warmer too! (She shivers.) I'm nearly frozen.

LUCY: Ain't this gale terrific? You'd of thought it was March, wouldn't you, miss? I'm just now buildin' up the fire. (She pokes the fire.) Tell me, miss—how was Miss Maggie's weddin'?

FLEDA: Lovely, Lucy—perfectly lovely. Very quiet but very sweet.

LUCY: Champagne?

FLEDA (*laughing*): Oh, yes! My father kept brilliant on one bottle!

LUCY (*turning from the fire*): Now, ain't that nice! Well, miss, I guess I'd better go tell the lady you're here. (*She starts to go.*) She's been powerful anxious— (*She breaks off suddenly as she sees* MRS. GERETH *entering from the hall.*)

MRS. GERETH: Fleda, darling! Welcome to poor little Ricks!

FLEDA (*coming forward*): Mrs. Gereth!

(*The two women embrace.*)

MRS. GERETH: You got my telegram?

FLEDA: Last night—in West Kensington.

(LUCY *goes out, closing the double doors behind her.*)

MRS. GERETH (*wearily*): I've been wanting awfully to see you. You're the only one who really understands. You don't understand *everything*, of course, but of all my friends you're far away the least stupid. And now—with nothing else but my four walls—at least you'll be a bit of furniture. (*She laughs.*) I've always taken you for that, you know—one of my very best finds. (*She glances about the room with contemptuous disdain.*) Isn't this little place horrid? It's almost as bad as Waterbath! (*Woefully*) How in the world could a country house three miles from a railroad station look so utterly, utterly suburban?

FLEDA (*pleasantly*): Mrs. Gereth, you may turn me out of the house for saying so, but there's not a woman in England who wouldn't feel privileged to live here. Where on earth did you find these beautiful things?

MRS. GERETH: Beautiful things! Why, they're the wretched things that were already here—that stupid starved old woman's. (*She pauses to adjust slightly the position of a chair.*)

FLEDA: The maiden aunt's, you mean? The nicest, dearest old lady who ever lived? But I thought you'd quite exterminated the maiden aunt.

MRS. GERETH: Oh, she was stored in an empty barn—stuck away for a sale. I simply fished her out again.

FLEDA: You simply made a *delight* of her! (*She moves about the room, admiring its beauties.*) These tender little telltale things— don't they find a way to your heart? It's not the great chorus of Poynton, but surely you don't insist on *that!* (*With almost lyrical intensity*) It's a voice so gentle, so human, so feminine—you must have heard it unawares—else you'd never have made this room so perfect. It's your special genius, my dear—you've only to be in a place a day or two with four sticks for something to come of it.

MRS. GERETH: Well, darling, if anything *has* come of it here, it's come of exactly four! (*She pauses to straighten a picture.*) That's all there are—by the inventory!

FLEDA: Anything more would be too much. Anything more would spoil the mood—that delicate poetry of something dreamed and missed, of something *gone.* There's something here that will never be in the inventory!

MRS. GERETH (*bitterly*): Does it happen to be in your power to give it a name?

FLEDA: I could give it a dozen. It's a kind of fourth dimension. It's a presence—a perfume—a touch. It's a soul—a story—a life. There's ever so much more here than you and I!

MRS. GERETH (*derisively*): Oh, if you count the ghosts—!

FLEDA: Of course I count the ghosts! It seems to me ghosts count double—for what they *were* and for what they *are.* Somehow there were no ghosts at Poynton. That was the only fault— Poynton was too splendidly happy. Now, of course, there'll be a ghost or two…. You've really sent back everything?

MRS. GERETH: Literally everything—down to the last little miniature on the last little screen.

FLEDA: Even the Maltese cross?

MRS. GERETH: Why not that along with everything else? Especially since you like it so.

FLEDA: But you must be ready to drop!

MRS. GERETH (*sadly*): I'm very, very tired. I almost don't care.
I couldn't do it again.

FLEDA: I doubt if they'd *bear* it again!

MRS. GERETH: Oh, *they'd* bear it if *I* could! For *you* I *could*—for
you I *can still.* Nothing matters so long as *she's* not there.

FLEDA: And what if she *is* there—what if she's there already?

MRS. GERETH (*suddenly aroused*): Do you mean to tell me—at
an hour like this—you've really lost him?

FLEDA: I don't know, Mrs. Gereth. How can I say? I've not seen
him for so long—I don't even know where he is.

MRS. GERETH (*angrily*): Then you ought to be ashamed of
yourself—you and Owen both!

FLEDA: Please don't blame Owen. He'd have been with me
every day if I'd agreed. But I told him I'd see him again only
when he's able to show me his release from Mona—signed and
sealed. He *can't* yet, don't you see? That's why he hasn't been
back. But when he *does* come he'll be tremendously moved by the
wonderful thing you've done. (*With great earnestness*) I don't think
you really know him, Mrs. Gereth. He's ever so much cleverer
than he seems—he's remarkable in his own shy way. I love him so
much I'd die for him—I love him so much it's horrible. I haven't
a rag of pride left—I used to have, but it's gone. If Owen doesn't
know there isn't an inch of me that isn't his—! It's idiotic—it's
strange; and the strangest part of all is it isn't even happiness.
It's agony—it was from the first. But he's so kind it makes up for
everything.

MRS. GERETH (*with rising wrath*): Is it part of his kindness never
to come near you? Is it part of his kindness to leave you without
an inkling of where he is? Is it part of his kindness that after I've
toiled for six days, with my own weak hands, to denude myself in
your interest—so that I've nothing left but what's on my back—is
it part of his kindness that you can't even produce him for me?

FLEDA: Don't blame *him*, Mrs. Gereth! He'd do anything on
earth for me! It was I who sent him back to her. I refused to see
him again—except on another footing.

MRS. GERETH (*angrily*): *What* other footing?

FLEDA: Why, having it from *her* in black and white that she freely gives him up.

MRS. GERETH (*furiously*): Then you think he lies when he tells you he's free?

FLEDA: He's enough in love with me for anything!

MRS. GERETH (*savagely*): For anything, apparently, except to act like a man and impose his will on your incredible folly! For anything except to put an end to your systematic, idiotic perversity! After all, my dear, who *are* you, I'd like to know, that a gentleman who offers you what Owen offers should have to meet such sweet little scruples? I don't know what to *think* of him! I don't know what to *call* him! I'm so ashamed of him I can scarcely speak of him even to *you*. If Owen had the ghost of a sense of humour he'd have snapped his fingers at your refinements. Anyone but a jackass would have tucked you under his arm and marched you straight off to the Registrar!

FLEDA: To the *Registrar!*

MRS. GERETH (*her rage reaching white heat*): *That* would have been the *sane* thing to do. With a grain of gumption you'd both have felt it. *I'd* have found a way to take you if *I'd* been what Owen's supposed to be. Good God, girl—your place was to stand before me as a woman honestly married! You must excuse my saying you're literally unpleasant to me as you stand there now.

FLEDA: I'll go up to town at once.

MRS. GERETH (*with superb sarcasm*): Now? And pray who's to take you? Do you really mean you can't put your hand on him? *Find* him for me, you fool—*find* him for me!

FLEDA (*dismally*): What do you *want* with him, feeling the way you do to both of us?

MRS. GERETH (*wildly*): Never mind how I feel, and never mind what I say when I'm furious! Of course I cling to you both—you wretches—else I wouldn't suffer as I do. What I want of him is to see that he takes *you*. Come straight to town with me and try at least to get *at* him!

FLEDA: How can I get *at* him? He'll come when he's ready.

MRS. GERETH (*with high contempt*): Ready for what? Ready to see me ruined?

FLEDA (*gently*): Please, Mrs. Gereth—don't be cruel to me. I'm very unhappy. I don't see why you take for granted Owen's "lost."

MRS. GERETH: If he's not lost why are you unhappy?

FLEDA (*almost in tears*): I'm unhappy because I torment you and you don't understand me.

MRS. GERETH: No, Fleda, I *don't* understand you. I don't understand you at all. It's just as if you and Owen were of quite another race. You make me feel very old-fashioned and simple and bad. But you'll have to take me as I am, since you take so much else *with* me! (*Bitterly*) It would have been better for me if I'd never known you, and certainly better if I'd never taken such a fancy to you. But that was all my own doing—you didn't run after me. I pounced on you and caught you up. You're a stiff little beggar, my dear, in spite of your pretty manners. It was your sympathy that did it—your beautiful feeling for those damned spoils. You were sharper about them than anyone I'd ever known. Well! You see where it's landed us!

FLEDA: If you'll go for him yourself, I'll wait here.

MRS. GERETH: To Colonel Gereth's, you mean?

FLEDA: Doesn't he stay there when he's in town?

MRS. GERETH (*angrily*): How should *I* know—with my wretched relations with him? I haven't heard a word from Owen in nearly two months!

FLEDA: But wasn't it that very silence that made you think everything's at an end between them?

MRS. GERETH (*with renewed violence*): Deuce take you, Fleda! First you tell me Owen cares for you, and then in the same breath you say he's probably at Waterbath. Pardon me if I'm so dull I don't see my way in such darkness. If he's at Waterbath he doesn't care for you. If he cares for you he's not at Waterbath.

FLEDA: Then where *is* he?

MRS. GERETH (*furiously*): Isn't that a question for you to *answer* rather than *ask?*

FLEDA: Oh, Mrs. Gereth! You simplify too much. You always did and you always will. The tangle of life is much more intricate than you've ever felt it to be. You slash into it with a great pair of shears—as if you were one of the Fates! If Owen's at Waterbath he's there to wind everything up!

MRS. GERETH (*shaking her head*): You don't believe a word you're saying. I've frightened you—just as you've frightened me. You're whistling in the dark to keep up your courage. I can only repeat—you're beyond me. Your perversity's a thing to howl over. (*Her voice breaking*) Owen I can just make out, for Owen *is* a blockhead. (*With quiet, tragic finality*) Yes, Owen's a blockhead. He's disgustingly weak—I don't see why you try to cover it up.

FLEDA (*simply*): Because I love him. It's because he's weak that he needs me.

MRS. GERETH: *That* was why his father needed *me*. And *I* didn't fail his father! (*She gives* FLEDA *time to appreciate this remark.*) Mona Brigstock isn't weak. She's stronger than you!

FLEDA: I never thought she was weak.

MRS. GERETH: I *did* tell you to let yourself go, but it's plain enough you really haven't. If Mona's got him—if Mona's got him, it'll be plain enough *she has!*

FLEDA: Come—let's look for him together. They may know something about him at Colonel Gereth's. But first I'd better wire to Waterbath.

MRS. GERETH: In *your* name?

FLEDA: Of course. (*She seats herself at the desk and proceeds to write out a telegram.*)

MRS. GERETH: But wouldn't it be better to see if we can't make out his whereabouts first?

FLEDA: Why so? It'll always be so much done. And certainly I don't mind the shilling.

MRS. GERETH: The shilling's *my* shilling!

FLEDA: Oh, no—I'm superstitious. To succeed it must be all *me!*

MRS. GERETH: Well, if *that'll* make it succeed! In any case, since he's probably not there—

FLEDA: If he's not there, then no harm's done. The Brigstocks will simply send it on.

MRS. GERETH: They'll read it first—I warrant Mona will! She'll keep it as proof of your immodesty!

FLEDA (*rising from the desk*): What of that?

MRS. GERETH: You don't mind her seeing it?

FLEDA: I don't mind anything. (*She reads the telegram.*) "I send this to Waterbath, on the possibility of your being there, to ask you to come to me."

MRS. GERETH (*taking the telegram and reading it*): But why have you given Maggie's address for a reply?

FLEDA: Because if he *does* come to me, he must come to me there. If that telegram goes, I return to Maggie's tonight.

MRS. GERETH: You won't receive him here with me? (*She rings for* LUCY.)

FLEDA (*firmly*): Absolutely not.

MRS. GERETH: Then won't you make your message a little stronger?

FLEDA: He'll come if he can.

MRS. GERETH: But suppose—suppose we've already lost?

FLEDA (*simply*): It will be very hard.

MRS. GERETH: But you'll still come abroad with me?

FLEDA: If you still want me. It'll seem very strange if you do.

MRS. GERETH: I'll need your company. As time goes on we can always talk of the spoils.

FLEDA: The spoils? (*She smiles sadly.*) Never! Never!

(LUCY *enters carrying a newspaper and a letter.*)

MRS. GERETH: Take this telegram, Lucy, and see that John gets it to the post office at once. (*She hands the telegram to* LUCY.)

LUCY: Yes, mum. *The Mornin' Post*, mum. (*She places* The Morning Post *on the table.* MRS. GERETH *snatches it up wildly, sits down on the sofa, and leafs desperately through its pages.*) And a letter for you, miss. (*She hands the letter to* FLEDA.)

FLEDA: For me? But who even knows I'm here?

LUCY: Looks to me like Mr. Owen's hand, miss.

(FLEDA *is about to open the letter when a piercing cry of agony and doom comes from* MRS. GERETH. *Both* FLEDA *and* LUCY *are struck motionless.*)

MRS. GERETH (*looking up from her newspaper*): He's done it! He's done it! (*Her eyes meet* FLEDA*'s.*) It's the end.

FLEDA: They're married?

MRS. GERETH: They're married. (*She returns for a moment to the newspaper, then suddenly looks up.*) Deep in my heart I've always known he'd marry a frump!

FLEDA (*with calm self-possession*): The fact that he's done it—the very fact that he couldn't *not* do it—shows how right I was. He was bound to Mona by an obligation he couldn't break.

MRS. GERETH (*rising from the sofa*): What sort of obligation do you call that? No such obligation exists for an instant between any man and any woman who have hatred on one side. He ended by hating her, and now he probably hates her more than ever. (*She snatches the telegram from* LUCY*'s hand, tears it up violently, and throws the pieces in the fire.*) There! (*She rubs her hands.*) So much for Mona Brigstock! The flames will finish *her!* (*She turns to* FLEDA.) Well, haven't you anything to say? Are you pretending you don't care?

(LUCY *goes out, leaving the double doors open.*)

FLEDA: I'm trying not to think of myself.

MRS. GERETH: If you're thinking of Owen, how can you *bear* to think?

FLEDA (*almost in tears*): I can't—I can't! I don't understand!

MRS. GERETH: Well, *I* do! There was no obligation, as you call it, when you saw him last—in this room—when you sent him back to *her*—hating her as he did.

FLEDA: If he went, doesn't that prove he recognized an obligation?

MRS. GERETH: He recognized rot! You know what *I* think of him. All I can say is—he took strange ways to please you! There was no obligation till suddenly the situation changed.

FLEDA: Suddenly?

MRS. GERETH: Mona must have heard I was sending back the things. I sent them for *you*, but it was *her* I touched.

FLEDA (*with cool revulsion, half to herself*): Mona?

MRS. GERETH: And why not? She's a brute! *She* did what *you wouldn't.* She took steps—powerful steps. And before he could turn around he was married!

FLEDA: At that place you spoke of in town?

MRS. GERETH (*contemptuously*): At a registry office—like a pair of low atheists! (*She glances at the newspaper.*) They're to be publicly married on the twenty-second at Waterbath Church—with three clergymen, fourteen bridesmaids, and a special train from town.

FLEDA: When do they move to—to Poynton?

MRS. GERETH: Not till after the public marriage. I suppose she'll live there alone.

FLEDA: Alone?

MRS. GERETH: She'll have it all to herself.

FLEDA: How do you know?

MRS. GERETH: Oh, *he'd* never live with *that* creature. Never! But just the same *she's* his wife, and *you're* not! (*She glances at the newspaper.*) Ah! I see *they* plan to go abroad. (*She reads.*) "According to reports of several friends, Mr. and Mrs. Owen Gereth, of Poynton Park, propose spending the winter months in Paris." (*She looks up from the newspaper.*) Then apparently he *is* living with her!

FLEDA: Surely it's the only proper thing to do.

MRS. GERETH: They're beyond me—I give it up.

(MRS. GERETH *folds up the newspaper and lays it aside with a gesture of finality. By now* FLEDA *has opened her letter and glanced over its contents.*)

FLEDA: *I* don't give it up—I never did.

MRS. GERETH: Then what do *you* make of his aversion to her?

FLEDA: Oh, she's dispelled it. I understand everything now—it's all very simple. Mona's upset by failure, but she blooms and expands with success. There was something she set her heart on—that house exactly as she saw it.

MRS. GERETH: She never saw it at all—she never looked at it!

FLEDA: She doesn't look with her eyes—she looks with her ears. In her own way she took it in. And when it was—despoiled, she naturally became disagreeable. But her attitude lasted only while the reason for it lasted.

MRS. GERETH: Go on—I can bear it now.

FLEDA: I know you can, or I shouldn't dream of speaking this way. From the moment the house was once more what it *had* been, Mona's natural charm reasserted itself.

MRS. GERETH (*with supreme sarcasm*): Her natural charm!

FLEDA: It's very great—everyone thinks so. There must be something in it.

MRS. GERETH: Your explanation would doubtless be perfect if Owen didn't love *you*.

FLEDA: What do *you* know about his "loving" me?

MRS. GERETH: I know what Mrs. Brigstock herself told me.

FLEDA: You never in your life took her word for anything else.

MRS. GERETH: Then won't *yours* do? Haven't I had it from your own lips that he cares for you?

FLEDA: Mrs. Gereth, you mix things up. I've only said *I* care for *him!*

MRS. GERETH: Well, my dear—don't think I'll be the least bit surprised when he comes back to make up to *you*.

FLEDA: He won't do that—not Owen!

MRS. GERETH: Why not? What does he say in his letter?

FLEDA: He says that he and Mona plan to spend the spring in southern France and then go on to Switzerland for the summer.

MRS. GERETH: Humph! Now that Mona has Poynton fast she's perfectly willing to live abroad. (*As if to go*) Well, my dear, that settles it. I'll stay where I am. And I'll expect *you* to stay with me. (*She is at the terrace door.*) Our only chance is the chance Mona may die.

FLEDA (*shaking her head*): Mona won't die.

MRS. GERETH: Well, *I* will—thank God! Till then— (*She pauses as if suddenly and dreadfully inspired.*) Till then, my dear, we're together. That's all we *are* now—it's all we have. (*She puts on her coat.*) It's all we have!

(MRS. GERETH *opens the terrace door and goes out, closing the door behind her. Alone at last,* FLEDA *turns to finish her letter. For a moment she reads to herself; then she begins reading aloud.*)

FLEDA (*reading*): "I should like you to have as a remembrance something of mine—something of real value—something from Poynton. I want you to choose for yourself the thing in the whole house that's most beautiful and precious. The people have complete instructions. They'll act for you in every possible way and put the whole place at your service. There's a thing Mummy used to call the Maltese cross, and that, I think I've heard her say, is very wonderful. Let me feel that I can trust you for this. You won't refuse if you'll simply think a little what it must be that makes me ask." (*She looks up.*) "What it must be that makes me ask...." (*Suddenly she is aware that someone has entered the room. Turning, she sees* OWEN *and springs up in astonishment.*) Owen Gereth! What on earth—?

OWEN (*smiling coolly*): Oh, I knew you'd be surprised to see *me*—especially now.

FLEDA: But where's Mona? Where's—?

OWEN (*casually*): Oh, Mona's in the library.

FLEDA (*stunned*): In the *library!*

OWEN: She didn't really want to come at all, of course. But we've been at Poynton all afternoon and—

FLEDA: Then you've come down to Poynton already!

OWEN: Oh, yes! Oh, yes!

FLEDA: But I thought you'd be off to Waterbath right away!

OWEN: We *were* to be off last night. But first Mona wanted to check on the things.

FLEDA (*drily*): And how did Mona *find* the things?

OWEN (*casually*): Oh, she found them all right.

FLEDA: All *right!*

OWEN: Of course there'll have to be a few changes. Next year, when we get back from Switzerland, Mona plans to turn the library into a billiard room. And later on—as part of our wedding gift—Mrs. Brigstock hopes to make a grand ballroom out of the west chapel.

FLEDA: So Mrs. Brigstock came along too?

OWEN (*abashed*): Well, Mona doesn't like to travel alone.

FLEDA: Then I presume Mrs. Brigstock plans to join you two abroad?

OWEN: Oh, I *hope* not! She hasn't spoken of *that* yet. She's really been too busy with plans for the public wedding.

FLEDA: Oh, yes—we've just been reading *The Morning Post.*

OWEN: You and Mummy? How does *she* take it?

FLEDA: She takes it very hard. Very hard. She's gone for a walk in Poynton Park. You must have just missed her as you came up.

OWEN: Then I'm glad I didn't miss *you.* In fact, that's really why I came.

FLEDA (*astonished*): You came here to see *me?*

OWEN: To make sure you *understand.*

FLEDA: Understand?

OWEN (*with intimate familiarity*): Oh, you know what I mean— didn't you get my letter?

(*Suddenly* MRS. BRIGSTOCK *appears in the hall and strides into the room. She is even more extravagantly dressed than in Act Two. And if possible her manner is even more imperious. At her appearance* OWEN *is abruptly silenced.*)

MRS. BRIGSTOCK (*peremptorily*): Owen, I do think you'd better come along now. We mustn't miss our train. (*She looks about the room.*) Where is Mrs. Gereth? I thought— (*At last she sees* FLEDA.) Oh! Miss Vetch!

FLEDA (*simply*): Good afternoon, Mrs. Brigstock.

MRS. BRIGSTOCK (*ignoring* FLEDA): It's getting late, Owen—and besides, it's cold in that library.

OWEN: Then why don't you bring Mona in here by the fire?

MRS. BRIGSTOCK: In here? With—? (*She eyes* FLEDA *contemptuously as she turns to go.*)

OWEN (*starting to go*): I was just about to ask Miss Vetch to come down to Waterbath for the wedding.

MRS. BRIGSTOCK (*coldly*): Indeed.

(LUCY *is heard shouting offstage.*)

LUCY: Mrs. Gereth! Oh, Mrs. Gereth! (*She appears in the hall, breathless and wide-eyed.*) Oh, miss! Where's Mrs. Gereth? Quick! Poynton—Poynton—it's on fire!

FLEDA (*aghast*): Poynton—on fire!

LUCY: Burnin' fast, miss. Ain't it quite too dreadful?

FLEDA (*rushing to the terrace door*): Poynton? Poynton?

LUCY: Burnin' fast. And not a soul in charge but a pack o' clumsy servants—not the lady's lot, I warrant!

OWEN (*aghast*): Poynton!

LUCY: A nice job for caretakers! Some rotten old chimley, I s'pose—or one of them portable lamps set down in the wrong place. What's done it's this cruel, cruel gale. (*Turning to* FLEDA) Awkward for you, miss—I see!

FLEDA (*stunned*): You mean Poynton's *gone?*

LUCY: Must be near it by now, miss—with this awful gale. I was there myself not five minutes ago—the very first I'd heard of it. They were fightin' it then, but you couldn't say they'd got it down.

MRS. BRIGSTOCK (*frantically*): *Were they saving the things?*

LUCY: That's just it, mum—to get *at* the blessed things! And the want of right help—ain't it maddenin' to see 'em muff it so! This ain't a place, like, for nothin' organized. They don't come up to no *reel* emergency. (FLEDA *starts to go, but* LUCY *checks her.*) Oh, no, miss—don't do that! You won't care for it at all. Believe me, it ain't no place for a young lady!

FLEDA (*dazed*): You mean that great house is *lost?*

LUCY: Well, miss—what can you call it if it ain't rightly saved?

MRS. BRIGSTOCK (*dashing to the door in furious agitation*): Mona! (*She shouts desperately into the hall.*) Mona!

OWEN: Oh, God! What will Mona say? (*He follows* MRS. BRIGSTOCK *to the door.*) Mona! Mona!

(*By now* MRS. GERETH *is standing at the terrace door, her face white and expressionless, her voice cold and grim.*)

MRS. GERETH: Mona? Mona? Where is Mona? (*She moves slowly toward the hall door as the others stand motionless, staring at her in silence. Panting with intensity, she speaks as if in a trance.*) There's been a fire. Poynton's on fire! Hadn't we better tell Mona?

(*At the door* MRS. GERETH *turns to look across the room at the lurid light of the evening sky, aglow with the flames of Poynton. Then she turns to meet* MONA *in the hall as the curtain slowly falls.*)

A Note on the Author

ROBERT MANSON MYERS, educator, historian, playwright, and literary critic, is Professor of English Emeritus at the University of Maryland. He graduated *summa cum laude* from Vanderbilt University and received graduate degrees from Columbia University and Harvard University. After teaching at Yale University, The College of William and Mary, and Tulane University, he was Fulbright Research Scholar at The University of London and Fulbright Visiting Professor at The University of Rotterdam.

Dr. Myers's plays have been staged on both sides of the Atlantic and aired on the BBC. His numerous books include two works on the composer Handel and the classic spoof, *From Beowulf to Virginia Woolf: An Astounding and Wholly Unauthorized History of English Literature*. His best-selling Civil War epic, *The Children of Pride*, widely acclaimed as "The American *War and Peace*," won the coveted Carey-Thomas Award in 1972 and the prestigious National Book Award in 1973.